Tongues

God's Provision for Dynamic Growth
and Supernatural Living

Patricia King

Tongues

Tongues is a supernatural gift of the Spirit which enables believers in Jesus to speak in a heavenly language that they do not understand with their natural mind.

"These signs will accompany those who have believed: in My name they will cast out demons, they will speak with new tongues" Mark 16:17.

ISBN 978-1-936101-46-7

Distributed by Patricia King Ministries
P. O. Box 1017
Maricopa, Arizona 85139
PatriciaKing.com

Printed in the United States of America

Contents

Chapter 1

WHY IS THE HOLY SPIRIT IMPORTANT?

Would you be interested in receiving a key that would unlock the power of God within you ... accelerate your growth and maturity as a believer ... enable you to love the unlovable ... invite you to experience things of God that seem impossible to the average person ... and help you enjoy deepened intimacy with the Lord? I am sure you are saying, "Yes Ma'am, bring it on!"

This book offers insight concerning that key. All of the above-mentioned benefits and more are available to you in the person of the Holy Spirit. He wants to fill you afresh, leading and guiding you into a revelation of Christ that will transform your life. The Holy Spirit is an amazing Person who is fully committed to helping you become the individual God created you to be. In 1976, I became a brand new creation in Christ. I was saved, filled with the Holy Spirit, and blessed with tongues, a life-empowering gift from God, during a three-day period that changed my life forever.

COMING TO KNOW THE HOLY SPIRIT AND HIS GIFTS

I was born again in an Anglican church during the Charismatic Renewal. Being new to the church, I did not understand that "speaking in tongues" was so controversial. If they did not want me to speak in tongues, they should have locked me up the first few months I was a Christian. Only three days after receiving Christ, I was baptized with the Holy Spirit and spoke in tongues. This Anglican church had a number of people fired up for God who had been filled with the Spirit and spoke in tongues. However, many in the church questioned it and considered it, at the least, odd. I guess I was a problem for them; I was loud and enthusiastic. I did not know we were supposed to be quiet about receiving this exciting gift – they told me much too late.

After being baptized in the Holy Spirit, I became aware of a curious thing. They had two services on Sunday. They called their morning service the "*normal* service" and the evening service was the "*charismatic* service." I attended both every week and enjoyed their different flavors. But after reading Acts, chapter 2, I realized that normal for them was different from what the early church considered normal. I thought: *There is something really wrong with this picture!* We charismatics were instructed to be very careful – we tiptoed around the issue of "tongues" because, after all, we should not be offensive to the *normal* Christians. They labeled us peculiar, when in reality *we* were the normal ones.

COMING OF THE COMFORTER

When Jesus was about to leave earth, He told His disciples about the Person who would come after Him, One who would instruct and comfort them. For about three years, Jesus had lived night and day with His disciples: teaching them, explaining spiritual truth, and showing them healings and supernatural works. When His departure was near, Jesus explained about the Other, the Person who would take His place – the Holy Spirit.

The disciples were grief-stricken as Jesus talked about going away, so He reassured them:

> I tell you the truth, it is to your advantage that I go away; for if I do not go away, the Helper will not come to you; but if I go, I will send Him to you ... I have many more things to say to you, but you cannot bear them now. But when He, the Spirit of Truth, comes, He will guide you into all the truth; for He will not speak on His own initiative, but whatever He hears, He will speak; and He will disclose to you what is to come. He will glorify Me, for He will take of Mine and will disclose it to you. All things that the Father has are Mine; therefore I said that He takes of Mine and will disclose it to you (John 16:7,12-15).

In an earlier chapter of John, Jesus made the disciples an amazing promise: He said that after He left, they would do the same works He had done, and perform even "greater works" because He was going to His Father (John 14:12). Now, the works Jesus had done would no longer be confined to one person in one place; rather, they would be reproduced by the saints throughout the earth. First, however, Jesus instructed them to wait for the promised Holy Spirit.

His followers did as He told them. They waited prayerfully in the Upper Room for the Holy Spirit to come with power as Jesus had promised. Having seen firsthand through the example of Jesus how a spirit-empowered person could live, they longed for this infusion of God's power. Luke writes,

> These all with one mind were continually devoting themselves to prayer, along with the women, and Mary the mother of Jesus, and with his brothers (Acts 1:14).

Day one, they waited ... day two, they waited ... day three, they waited, and continued to wait ten days for the coming of the Holy Spirit. On the Jewish feast called the Day of Pentecost, the promise was fulfilled. We do not know how many were there on the first day, but on day ten, 120 faithful people received the gift of God – the baptism of the Holy Spirit! It was an incredible event unlike anything seen before on earth. Luke describes it in detail in Acts, chapter 2:

When the day of Pentecost had come, they were all together in one place. And suddenly there came from heaven a noise like a violent rushing wind, and it filled the whole house where they were sitting. And there appeared to them tongues as of fire distributing themselves, and they rested on each one of them. And they were all filled with the Holy Spirit and began to speak with other tongues, as the Spirit was giving them utterance (Acts 2:1-4).

The Holy Spirit was sent to empower you to be like Jesus and to do even "greater works" than He did.

THE HOLY SPIRIT AT SALVATION

When you become born again, the Holy Spirit takes up residence in you. However, this is only the beginning; God has much more for you. The moment you make Christ your personal Savior, His blood that was shed for your sins seals you into a covenant relationship with God. You become adopted into His family, His dearly loved child! When Jesus comes into your heart, the Spirit of God takes up residence within your reborn, human spirit. We are a spirit, we have a soul, and we live in a physical body – so when we are born-again, the Holy Spirit intertwines with our reborn, human spirit to become the "temple of God" (see 1 Corinthians 3:16).

> *The Holy Spirit was sent to empower you to be like Jesus and to do even "greater works" than He did.*

Jesus explained to Nicodemus that he must be "born of the Spirit" to experience the new birth. Nicodemus did not understand and asked how he could go back into his mother's womb to be born a second time. Jesus then said to him, "Truly, truly, I say to you, unless one is born of water and the Spirit he cannot enter into the kingdom of God. That which is born of the flesh is flesh, and that which is born of the Spirit is spirit" (John 3:5-6). He was saying, "Nicodemus, at your natural birth, you were born of the flesh; but to enter into the Kingdom, you must be born of the Spirit."

When we are born-again, the Spirit of God is living inside us. When we receive the baptism in the Spirit, we receive an increase in God's power and authority to be a witness, as well as the ability to accomplish our God-given purpose.

Since we have the Spirit of God living on the inside of us, we possess everything that we will ever need in life, because He is the Giver of Life. When we have the Author of Life living within us, we are able to overcome anything that may come against us. John said, "For whatever is born of God overcomes the world; and this is the victory that has overcome the world – our faith" (1 John 5:4). We can overcome everything the world throws at us because we have the Overcomer residing within us.

Peter further explains in 2 Peter 1:2-3:

His divine power has granted to us everything pertaining to life and godliness, through the true knowledge of Him who called us by His own glory and excellence.

When we receive the Baptism in the Spirit, we receive an increase in God's power and authority to be a witness, as well as the ability to accomplish our God-given purpose.

Scripture also says that when you are born again you become a brand new creation; old things pass away and everything becomes new (see 2 Corinthians 5:17). This is a miracle of God! It means that within your spirit, you have *new life*. Not only are you born into the Kingdom of God but the Kingdom is born in you, and the kind of life God experiences is inside you. You are not just going to receive eternal life some time in the future, you possess it now – it *already* resides in you!

When you stand before the Father, He does not see your past sins and present shortcomings, or future mistakes – He sees Christ in you. The power and the Spirit of God are within you, the Kingdom of God is in you, and God has given you everything that is required for life and godliness (see 2 Peter 1:3).

> *When we receive the Baptism in the Spirit, we receive an increase in God's power and authority to be a witness, as well as the ability to accomplish our God-given purpose.*

Promise and Purpose of the Baptism of the Holy Spirit

Immediately following His Resurrection, Jesus breathed on His disciples, and the Bible says they received the Holy Spirit (see John 20:22). Yet, later as recorded in the book of Acts, Jesus told the disciples to wait for the promise of the Father, the baptism of the Holy Spirit. You might wonder why they needed to be baptized in the Spirit when they had already received Him.

The explanation is: when Jesus breathed on His disciples, they were born again, receiving the Spirit of God as they experienced the new birth. However, to be equipped with power to fulfill their purpose and carry the Good News to the known world, they needed more – the gift of the Holy Spirit – and so do you. Luke writes:

> [Jesus] commanded them not to leave Jerusalem, but to wait for what the Father had promised, "Which," He said, "you heard of from Me; for John baptized with water, but you will be baptized with the Holy Spirit not many days from now ... You will receive power when the Holy Spirit has come upon you; and you shall be My witnesses both in

Jerusalem, and in all Judea and Samaria, and even to the remotest part of the earth" (Acts 1:4-8).

Baptism in the Holy Spirit Is the Key to Power

This Baptism, like water baptism, is a total immersion in God's presence for the purpose of producing power. The apostles were to be totally submerged, completely marinated in God's presence, as the Holy Spirit came upon them. The Baptism in the Spirit enabled the disciples to do the same works Jesus did, and even "greater works" … and it will do the same for YOU!

What they received was not merely a nice little "feeling." The sound of the Holy Spirit's coming was like a tornado, and flames like fire signaled His arrival. We should also note, "They were *all* filled" (Acts 2:4 emphasis added). The Holy Spirit filled every person present – every man and every woman – and they *all* spoke in "tongues."

One of the major evidences of the baptism with the Holy Spirit found repeatedly throughout the book of Acts is "speaking in tongues" (see Acts 2:1–4; 10:44–48; 19:1–7). Being "Spirit filled" is, of course, an on-going relationship with God, not a one-time experience. However, I believe this "second experience," which is available to all believers, is vitally important and essential for all.

How did the people in Jerusalem know that something supernatural was happening? The crowd heard them all "speaking in tongues." People from many different nations heard the 120 people gathered in the Upper Room declare praises to God in their native tongues:

> *Speaking in tongues was normal for early believers, and that same gift is available for today's Christians, too.*

Now there were dwelling in Jerusalem Jews, devout men from every nation under heaven. And at this sound the multitude came together, and they were bewildered, because each one was hearing them speak in his own language. And they were amazed and astonished, saying, "Are not all these who are speaking Galileans? And how is it that we hear, each of us in his own native language? ... We hear them telling in our own tongues the mighty works of God." And all were amazed and perplexed, saying to one another, "What does this mean?" But others mocking said, "They are filled with new wine" (Acts 2:5–13).

What does this mean to present-day Christians?

Speaking in tongues was normal for *early* believers, and that same gift is available for *today's* Christians, too.

THE TRUTH ABOUT SPIRITUAL GIFTS

You might wonder, "If we have everything within us that we need for life and godliness, as the Bible says, then why do we fall short in so many areas? How do we get what is on the inside of us released for practical living and godliness?" It is not by attending ten years of Bible school or having a degree in religion from a college or seminary, although that can be beneficial. It is not even by serving in your local church, although that should be encouraged. The way we receive what we need for "life and godliness" is by FAITH ... and faith alone. The God-given potential residing within you is only released through faith.

I see *new* Christians walk in power by their faith – leading people to Christ, healing the sick and experiencing miracles, signs, and wonders. Their results are not because they are special or have a greater measure of maturity in Christ but because they have the *faith* to release the power of the Holy Spirit inside them. Every Christian is special; each one is precious to God and every one can operate in these gifts by faith. However, you have to be bold, and risk failure. Someone once said that "faith is spelled: R-I-S-K."

Remember, *every* believer can operate in all nine gifts of the Spirit. The gifts are inherent in the Holy Spirit. If He is in you so also are His gifts. YOU can function in all nine gifts if the Spirit dwells within you. YOU can speak in tongues.

ACTIVATE WHAT IS WITHIN

The gift of tongues is one you already possess within, because it pertains to "life and godliness."

Even if you do not presently speak in tongues, you already possess this incredible gift because the Holy Spirit lives within you.

Even though tongues may not yet be manifested, that does not mean you do not have it. Not perceiving a thing does not imply it is not there. It only means the gift is not in use because it has not yet been activated.

Paul wrote an apostolic letter to the chaotic church in Corinth with instructions for bringing things into divine order. He taught them about the Holy Spirit's gifts, operations, manifestations, and anointings for a local church. Paul explained:

> Now there are varieties of gifts, but the same Spirit. And there are varieties of ministries, and the same Lord. There are varieties of effects, but the same God who works all things in all persons. But to each one is given the manifestation of the Spirit for the common good (1 Corinthians 12:4–7).

Even if you do not presently speak in tongues, you already possess this incredible gift because the Holy Spirit lives within you.

According to Paul, each person is given a "manifestation of the Spirit for the common good." The Holy Spirit shows His presence and activity in a meeting through signs, wonders, miracles, and through the gifts of the Spirit. Imagine that I am standing in front of you with a piece of paper hidden behind my back. The paper is present but "concealed" by my body. However, when I bring the paper in front, you see it; it is "manifested."

The Holy Spirit's presence is always around us. Theologians call this the "Omnipresence of God" – He is present everywhere, all the time (see Psalm 139:7–12). However, there are times when the Holy Spirit reveals Himself in a greater measure. When He appears through the gifts of the Spirit, operating in and through the people of God, He is manifesting and revealing Himself. This may be called the "manifest presence of God."

Paul lists nine unique gifts the Holy Spirit uses to manifest Himself when Christians assemble themselves together. The Spirit of God brings them forth:

+ The Word of Wisdom
+ The Word of Knowledge
+ Faith
+ Gifts of Healing

- Effecting of Miracles
- Prophecy
- Distinguishing of Spirits
- Various Kinds of Tongues
- Interpretation of Tongues

During a meeting of believers, someone might be inspired to bring forth a prophetic word, another person a message in tongues, another the interpretation of the tongues, and someone else might have a word of knowledge. We can operate in each of the gifts, as the Holy Spirit inspires us to do so and as we respond by faith, because it is the *same* Spirit working through all the gifts.

However, the next time we come together it might be a different type of meeting and God may choose to use the same or different people in the same or other gifts. The important point is this: when the Holy Spirit resides within, you have the Kingdom of God and *all* that you need – everything

> *You can speak in tongues, operate in other spiritual gifts and be released into your full potential!*

that pertains to life and godliness. A deep-down understanding of this truth will be life changing and enable you to "walk in the Spirit."

You can speak in tongues, operate in other spiritual gifts and be released into your full potential!

Chapter 2

WHY PRAY IN
TONGUES?

The truth is – you have the potential to speak in tongues and connect with God in ways you never dreamed possible. So, is it okay to desire to speak in tongues? Is it godly to desire the gifts of the Spirit? Can the desire to speak in tongues be a hunger placed in us by God? What does God's Word say about desiring this gift?

YOUR JOB IS TO PURSUE LOVE
AND DESIRE SPIRITUAL GIFTS

Paul says – "Pursue love, yet desire earnestly spiritual gifts, but especially that you may prophesy" (1 Corinthians 14:1). Receiving spiritual gifts is not optional for Christians; it is a command. Paul goes on to say that if we operate in spiritual gifts without love, we are nothing but a "noisy gong or a clanging cymbal" (1 Corinthians 13:1–3).

We have to become people who allow the love of God to flood our hearts ... give back that love to God ... and lavish it on others.

The body of Christ has moved into an apostolic season, a time beyond having church as usual. God desires to restore the Church to the powerful, dynamic, influential force it once was! For that to happen, we *must* have the same power as the early church leaders who went forth from the Upper Room in the power of the Spirit. Paul said, "I'm not coming to you speaking with mere words of man's wisdom. I'm coming to you with a demonstration of power" (1 Corinthians 2:1–5, author's paraphrase). We need spiritual gifts; therefore, we must seek God until we receive, because we, too, need to operate in "demonstrations of power."

LUKE DESCRIBED HOW THE EARLY CHURCH OPERATED

And with great power the apostles were giving testimony to the resurrection of the Lord Jesus, and abundant grace was upon them all (Acts 4:33).

That is what we need – great power and abundant grace.

One reason for their powerful preaching of Jesus and mighty demonstrations of the Spirit is that they prayed in tongues – they had learned to connect with the power of the Spirit by praying in the Spirit.

When the Bible says in 1 Corinthians 14:1 to "desire earnestly spiritual gifts, but especially that you may prophesy," it is not saying that we should ignore the other spiritual gifts. No! We are to desire *all* the gifts of the Spirit with great passion, but aspire for the gift of prophecy more than the others because it is the most beneficial to the entire body of Christ. If by faith you joyfully strive to operate in these things, you will grow, develop, and be released into these gifts beyond your imagination.

In order to explain how important the gift of tongues is today, I have listed five of the many reasons to speak in tongues:

1. SPEAK MYSTERIES

The first reason to desire the gift of tongues is that when we pray in tongues, we are praying mysteries. "For one who speaks in a tongue does not speak to men but to God; for no one understands, but in his spirit he speaks mysteries" (1 Corinthians 14:2).

In other words, when you speak in tongues, you will not understand what you say, unless you receive an interpretation through the companion gift of Interpretation of Tongues. (An interpretation is not a word for word translation but the gist of what has been spoken in tongues.)

Some time ago, I was in a home-group meeting and began prophesying over people. When I came to one man, I felt led by God to speak in tongues first, before giving him a prophetic word. After the meeting, he told me, "I speak Aramaic; that's my natural language. When you were talking in tongues, you were speaking Aramaic." He had written down what I said in tongues, "Praise be to the glory of my Father." How awesome! Even though you do not know what you are saying, God is speaking mysteries through you!

Tongues open up the realm of kingdom mysteries not only concerning insights for individuals but concerning insights into the heart and ways of God that have not yet been revealed. It has been only 2,000 years since Christ lived and about 6,000 years since the creation of the earth; that short time could never contain all the knowledge God wants to reveal. There are still things God longs to proclaim to those who pray in the Spirit. When you pray in tongues, you are birthing from the spirit realm hidden revelation of the mysteries of Christ that will become manifest within the natural realm.

> *Mysteries need to be revealed*
> *at a given time and place.*
> *Never think you know*
> *all of God's mysteries.*

Jesus said to His disciples, "I have many more things to say to you, but you cannot bear them now. But when He, the Spirit of truth, comes, He will guide you into all the truth" (John 16:13).

Sometimes when I am stuck and do not know the answer for breakthrough, I pray in tongues for a while and often, as I am praying or soon after, the answer is revealed. Tongues unlock the mysteries and secrets of God.

The secret things belong to the Lord our God, but the things revealed belong to us and to our sons forever (Deuteronomy 29:29).

2. Edify Your Spirit

The second reason to speak in tongues is to edify (meaning to build up, construct, or raise) your spirit man. Paul explains: "One who speaks in a tongue edifies himself; but one who prophesies edifies the church. Now I wish that you all spoke in tongues" (1 Corinthians 14:4–5).

Contrary to what some people believe, Paul was not devaluing tongues in this Scripture, but was emphasizing prophecy in public gatherings. He was not saying that we should *not* speak in tongues or that they have no value in the believer's life. Rather, he taught that we are to pray in tongues as much as we can, in private, to build ourselves up.

You cannot take someone to a higher place (spiritually) than where you are. By building yourself up with tongues, you gain spiritual maturity and insight to build others up through prophecy.

3. Produce Deliverance and Breakthrough

The third reason for desiring tongues is for deliverance and breakthrough. If anything tries to steal from you the "abundant life" Jesus promised, you do not have to allow it. For example, you do not have to permit depression to dominate you.

Depression used to come on me every winter and make me miserable for three months; I

> *By building yourself up with tongues, you gain spiritual maturity and insight to build up others through prophecy.*

could sense it coming, and felt prison bars of doom and gloom being created. (That was before I became a Christian and learned depression could be overcome.)

Yet, even after becoming a Christian, I still suffered depression because I did not understand that I had power over Satan with authority to overcome. One day, as depression was attempting to grip me, I said to myself, "Oh no! There it is again." Then I heard God ask, "Do you want to be delivered from that?"

Surprisingly, I was not sure I wanted deliverance. I realized that, in some strange way, I liked the depression because people were much nicer to me when I was depressed. However, when I recognized that I had to give it up, the Lord said, "I will deliver you from depression if you desire Me to."

I replied, "Lord, I really do want to be free."

He said, you have the power to overcome depression. I have given you power over all the power of the enemy but you must exercise that

Bind your mind to truth instead of facts.

power and resist the lies of the devil." Depression is a lie! It is not the truth.

Facts vs. Truth

"Facts" and "truths" are completely different. Facts belong to the earthly realm but truths belong to the eternal realm — eternal truths always triumph over earthly facts. While facts are accurate in the realm of time, facts can also contradict the eternal truth and be lies.

You cannot allow yourself to embrace facts over truths — you should acknowledge facts, if they are accurate, but refuse to allow them to rule over the Truth.

For instance, you can acknowledge the fact that you have headache symptoms, but you do not have to accept it because there is a higher truth. You can resist the headache because God's truth is contrary to the fact. The Bible says you are healed by the stripes of Jesus (see Isaiah 53:4 and Matthew 8:14-17).

Bind your mind to truth instead of facts.

The Lord taught me how to overcome depression through a vision of a mail carrier bringing a package of depression to my front door. The postman said, "Here's your depression." The sender was Lu-C-Fer. In this vision, I saw myself write across the package, "Return to Sender." The Lord warned me, "Do not let that package into your house (your life); don't sign for it; don't suck it in or in anyway receive it ... RESIST!"

After the vision, I went for a ten-mile prayer walk. I prayed in tongues almost the entire time while resisting feelings of depression. I was firm in my commitment to stand in truth and resist the devil so he would flee in terror. Soon, I felt depression lift, and that day back in 1980 was the last time I suffered from depression.

Of course, it knocked on the door of my mind from time to time, but I would do exactly what God taught me, refuse to receive it and write across the package of temptation, "RETURN TO SENDER" in bold letters. Then, I would pray in tongues until I felt the pressure of the temptation leave. Depression is not in heaven and, as a child of God, you are not required to endure it on earth. Speaking in tongues builds you up to resist the enemy and frees you from satanic attacks and addictions.

> *God can bring tremendous breakthroughs in our lives through praying in tongues, because we are praying the "will of God."*

God can bring tremendous breakthrough in our lives through praying in tongues, because we are praying the "will of God." When we engage in this gift, the supernatural element of praying in the Spirit is often more effective than praying only in our native language. God is supernatural, and through supernatural prayer He brings about change in our hearts and lives.

4. FIND HELP FOR WEAKNESSES

If the three previous reasons for praying in the Spirit were the only benefits, they would certainly be enough. However, the point of praying in tongues is to partner with the Holy Spirit to bring God's will to earth.

Paul considered it important to pray both in the Spirit and with understanding:

If I pray in a tongue, my spirit prays, but my mind is unfruitful. What is the outcome then? I will pray with the spirit and I will pray with the mind also; I will sing with the spirit and I will sing with the mind also (1 Corinthians 14:13–15).

We *pray with understanding* for things we comprehend with our natural mind and for those things we are unsure how best to pray, *we pray with the Spirit.* It is vital to engage in both types of prayer:

In the same way the Spirit also helps our weakness; for we do not know how to pray as we should, but the Spirit Himself intercedes for us with groanings too deep for words; and He who searches the hearts knows what the mind of the Spirit is, because He intercedes for the saints according to the will of God (Romans 8:26–27).

Paul also says that we groan for spiritual maturity:

And not only this, but also we ourselves, having the first fruits of the Spirit, even we ourselves groan within ourselves, waiting eagerly for our adoption as sons, the redemption of our body (Romans 8:23).

In this context, *groaning* signifies, "not having the words to convey a thing, a sound beyond human words." This is the Spirit interceding for us to become mature sons and daughters. The Holy Spirit is removing our childish ways, our weaknesses, and collaborating with us to become ever more of what God intended by interceding through us.

There is something inside your heart that cries out to God, "I want to be mature in You ... I want to see You better ... I want to know You more ... I want to be closer to You ... I want to take my place in what You are doing in the earth."

The Holy Spirit will help you pray in ways that would be impossible otherwise, because He prays the perfect will of God through you, often expressing things that cannot be uttered in mere human words.

When the Spirit is praying through us, it is also for others in the body of Christ. Paul said, "He intercedes for the saints according to the will of God" (Romans 8:27).

When you do not know how to pray for someone, by praying in tongues you can be certain you are praying according to God's will and know that your prayer will be answered.

This is the confidence which we have before Him, that, if we ask anything according to His will, He hears us. And if we know that He hears us in whatever we ask, we know that we have the requests which we have asked from Him (I John 5:14–15).

5. Keeping Yourself in God's Love

In Jude 20–21, we are taught that when we pray in the Spirit we are building ourselves up in our most holy faith, and as a result we keep ourselves in the love of God. Is love your greatest aim in life? When you pray in tongues, (which is one way of praying in the Holy Spirit), you are strengthened and kept in love. By praying in tongues, you receive an increased revelation of God's love for you and the power to demonstrate love to God and to those around you. As you pray in tongues, invite the Lord to increase your levels of love. He will.

Let love be your highest goal!
But you should also desire the special abilities the Spirit gives – especially the ability to prophesy
(1 Corinthians 14:1 NLT).

But you, dear friends, must build each other up in your most holy faith, pray in the power of the Holy Spirit (Jude 20 NLT).

Chapter 3

CAN TONGUES RELEASE REVIVAL?

When we pray in tongues, I believe we are preparing the next move of God, which will exceed our expectations and former outpourings. God said, "Be astonished! Wonder! Because I am doing something in your days – You would not believe it if you were told" (Habakkuk 1:5).

God wants to speak to us about the things He desires to do in the earth today. God's way is to reveal His will to us ... then we pray according to His revealed will ... and He brings it to pass on the earth. God collaborates with man in this way.

However, if we do not believe the things He reveals to our hearts, we cannot pray for what we do not believe. Unbelief would seem to create an insurmountable problem because it requires faith to release what God does. God has a strategy for getting us to pray in faith for His "seemingly unbelievable" will to be done on earth, and He reveals it to us in such a way that we can accept it.

I can imagine the Father telling the Spirit and the Son: "I know what I'll do. I'll give them a gift that contains My will as 'mysteries.' If I revealed to their natural minds what I'm about to do, they wouldn't pray for it because they couldn't believe in it. So I'll give them the gift of tongues, and as they pray by the Spirit in faith, I will reveal to their spirit man (not their mind) the mystery of what I'm about to do on the earth. Their prayers will create a landing place for my Kingdom to descend!"

> *God has a strategy for getting us to pray in faith for His "seemingly unbelievable" will to be done on earth, and He reveals it to us in such a way that we can accept it.*

Through praying in tongues, we prepare the next move of God and release it by faith.

WE ARE IN REVIVAL

Like me, you may have read about past revivals and wondered if revival can happen today. I believe it can. I have heard many reliable prophets say that revival is coming and that we will experience it soon. However, I have changed my way of talking about revival. I am no longer waiting for the next great revivalist or a new outpouring, I now say, "I *am* a revival looking for a place to happen because I carry revival within me." Revival is a Person and He lives in me – Jesus is Revival.

During the holiness revivals of the past, the "fear of the Lord" and conviction of sin were so strong that people would cry out for mercy. Entire cities and even nations were touched with the conviction and fear of the Lord as God poured out His Spirit.

The 1949 revival in the Hebrides strongly affected the surrounding area of Scotland. When the power of God came upon the people of the region, they shook under His presence and conviction. Even fishermen working miles offshore began shaking and crying out for God's mercy. God's Spirit touched the entire area and created ripples in regions beyond.

The revival meetings of Charles Finney were also characterized by a powerful conviction of the Holy Spirit. People became terrified during his meetings and they would cry out, "I've got to be saved!" He often replied, "You're not ready yet. The conviction for your sins has not yet gone deep enough. Come up here and sit in the 'anxious section." Sometimes they remained there for days until Finney believed they were ready to be born-again.

Finney was a man of prayer who birthed that revival on his knees in the forest. He set himself apart to God, praying, "God, You must visit me. You must come and transform me. Burn me up on the inside. Change me. I'm not leaving the forest until You show up." When God came, the fear of the Lord and the conviction of the Holy Spirit came upon him and dealt with him personally. Finney became so saturated with the essence of the fear of the Lord that when he walked into a building the convicting power of God's Spirit filled the place. When he visited a factory, the Spirit of conviction descended with such power that everyone began repenting of their sins. A powerful presence of God

43

was with him because of the many hours he spent in prayer.

Two thousand years ago, God poured out His Spirit – the Spirit of Revival is already here and it is in you! When speaking of the end times, God promised that the *"glory of the latter house"* would be greater than the former (see Haggai 2:9). Revival is here. In the coming days, rivers of revival will flow out of your innermost being in greater ways than has ever been witnessed on the earth. The world hasn't seen anything yet – the best is yet to come!

Revival is not coming, it is already *present*, living on the inside of you through the power of the Holy Spirit. By engaging God through praying in tongues, you can set revival fires ablaze and carry the Spirit of Revival with you.

YOU *CAN* "PRAY WITHOUT CEASING"

I want to give you a key that I have discovered for birthing revival – praying in tongues for several hours every day. I am not suggesting that you lock yourself in a room and pray for 12 hours each day; very few can do that. I am talking about learning to *"pray without ceasing"* (see 1 Thessalonians 5:17).

When you learn to pray all the time, no matter what you are doing, you can pray far more than you might think is possible.

When I was first saved and Spirit-filled, it was my privilege to be mentored by a wonderful woman of God named Mary Goddard, a "forerunner" in the Charismatic renewal. She guided me into the gifts of the Spirit and in other areas. She was a woman of grace, who knew the Holy Spirit and His gifts and allowed them to flow from her like a river. She was the founder of a ministry called Christian Services. Following her retirement in 1990, I became its overseer.

Attending her meetings was like sitting at the feet of Jesus for me, because His essence filled the room when she spoke. She taught the importance of praying in tongues. She would say, "You need to

> *Revival is already present, living on the inside of you through the power of the Holy Spirit. By engaging God through praying in tongues, you can set revival fires ablaze and carry the Spirit of Revival with you.*

charge your battery; you need to edify your spirit man." The secret of a successful Christian life is to "walk in the Spirit," and praying in the Spirit empowers us to walk in it. When we walk in the Spirit, we do what is pleasing to God, and the result of that focus is that we do not fulfill the lusts of the flesh!

She suggested we begin by praying an hour a day and promised that we would be edified in our inner man. She believed supernatural things would begin to happen to us. As soon as I returned home from that class, I could not wait to begin putting her advice into practice, and I started praying. After 15 minutes, I thought I had prayed four hours because it had been so much work. My flesh was resisting and I could not feel the anointing of God. I was wondering if anything was really happening as I prayed. However, I forced myself to keep on praying until my hour was up; it felt like I had prayed for ten hours.

The next day I tried it again. I kept recalling what Mary said, "You will be edified, and supernatural things will start to happen when you pray an hour a day in tongues." However, I did not *feel* "edified" after praying. Whatever it felt like to be edified, I was not experiencing it. Instead, I felt like I had fought a war for an entire hour; I was drained. Nevertheless, I continued to believe the Word that says you edify yourself when you pray in tongues. I thought, "Even though I don't feel edified, I'm going to keep doing it, because the Word says I need to."

I continued this every day, and sometimes would do two or three of those one-hour sessions of prayer in tongues. I began using every opportunity to pray in the Spirit: when in the shower, while cooking, as I walked down the street, even during vacuuming. I made it my goal to pray in the Spirit as many hours a day as I could manage.

In those early days, I prayed six to eight hours a day in tongues – yet never felt a thing. Soon, however, I noticed that divine appointments, miracles, prophetic revelations, and other manifestations of the supernatural were beginning to happen – but they always came *after* I had prayed, never *during* my prayer time.

The Lord taught me that if I continued to pray in tongues, His grace would come upon me. Grace is not only "undeserved favor" but it is also His divine influence upon your life. When you have His grace, you do not have to strive. His influence comes upon you, and you do His will effortlessly, without thinking and trying. It is as if you are being swept along in the flow of His peace and power.

You find yourself *in* the will of God ... *doing* the will of God ... *embracing* the will of God ... and *getting the fruit of* the will of God, all the while wondering, "How did I do that?" It is because grace is multiplied to you when you pray in tongues – *that* is the edification process. The Kingdom is not about your accomplishments; it is about the energizing work of the Holy Spirit in your life that enables you, through grace, to accomplish God's purposes.

If every person reading these words would begin praying in tongues for six to twelve hours a day, I believe we could birth in our world the revival that already dwells in us. We could release by faith, what we possess. It might not be *easy*, but I believe it is just that *simple*. The question is – will we do it? Can we commit to it?

> *If every person would begin praying in tongues for 6 to 12 hours a day, I believe we could birth in our world the revival that already dwells in us. The question is – will we do it? Can we commit to it?*

DEVELOPING A SENSITIVITY TO GOD'S VOICE

A shift is taking place in the body of Christ regarding the outpouring of His Spirit. *We* can shift things by praying in tongues because by doing so we release the supernatural into our world.

God has been telling me, "Go back and look at what happened in those years when you prayed in tongues every day for hour upon hour." When you are living life, things that happen may not seem unusual. However, in hindsight, you can often discern what God was doing.

Looking back, I see what God was birthing when I spent those hours praying in tongues: we had revival and a great harvest of souls. In those days, I would go for a walk after praying in tongues for a couple hours in the morning and I usually had the opportunity to lead two or three people to the Lord before lunch. It came easily and naturally, because God's Spirit was so readily available.

Praying in tongues causes your heart to become more sensitive to the voice of God. I remember one time driving home from shopping with my children in the backseat. While going up a hill, I passed a man walking along the street. I had prayed in

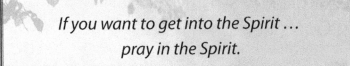

If you want to get into the Spirit ...
pray in the Spirit.

tongues for a couple of hours that morning and as I passed him, I heard the Holy Spirit say, "Stop, go back, and talk to that man."

I stopped, backed up, rolled down the window, and said, "Hi. This might sound strange, but I'm a Christian and while driving up the street the Holy Spirit told me to come back and tell you about God."

He said, "You're kidding."

I said, "No, He honestly said that to me."

He replied, "This is blowing my mind. While walking along just now, I was thinking about God, and decided to contact a friend who knows God. I was considering visiting her to ask some questions. Then you showed up." I led him to the Lord right there on the street. That kind of experience was normal for me – supernatural things like that happened continually.

When you pray in tongues for a couple hours a day, it will put you into a "zone of freedom" in the Holy Ghost. Over the years, I have learned many ways to pray and relate to God (soaking prayer, praying the Word, and prophetic intercession are just a few of them). I love them all, but lately the Holy Spirit has been reminding me of the importance of praying in tongues.

KEEPING YOU OUT OF YOUR HEAD

We do not connect with God with our mind but through our heart. Another benefit of praying in tongues is that it will "keep you out of your head." Scripture says that when you pray in tongues, your spirit is praying – your mind is not:

> For one who speaks in a tongue does not speak to men but to God; for no one understands, but in his spirit he speaks mysteries (1 Corinthians 14:2).

In other words, the mind does not know what you are saying as you pray with your spirit, and many times that is a great benefit.

FEAR OF ERROR

Another reason God is using tongues to birth His next outpouring is because He is revealing things today which could not have been understood in the past. Remember, Jesus told His disciples one reason for sending the Holy Spirit was:

> I have many more things to say to you, but you cannot bear them now. But when He, the Spirit of truth, comes, He will guide you into all the truth; for He will not speak on His own initiative, but whatever He hears, He will speak; and He will disclose to you what is to come (John 16:12–15).

You do not have to fear being led into false doctrine when you pray in the Spirit – He would never lead you into error because He is the Spirit of Truth. The main reason people get into error is that they follow their heads – they begin thinking about spiritual things with their mind rather than with their heart. They try to understand the supernatural with their natural, carnal mind.

The head is the "error center" for the body, the deception center. Sometimes when I speak of spiritual things from the Bible, people have said, "Oh, Patricia. You must be careful. You can get deceived with that kind of stuff." Deceived by the Bible? The only way to be deceived is to try to figure out spiritual things with carnal understanding.

Stay in relationship with God and with the Spirit of Truth, and you will never be led astray.

In the western church, we think that we must understand with our minds what God is doing before we can believe He is the One doing it. This approach never works. Paul warned that the natural man cannot comprehend the things of the Spirit of God. In fact, they are foolishness to him (See 1 Corinthians 2:14–16).

Today, we are in a spiritual revolution, like it or not; God is moving again and there is spiritual activity everywhere. Little children are having supernatural manifestations and visitations, which is mind boggling to those compelled to figure things out. Remember the odd thing Jesus said, in Luke 18:17:

> Truly I say to you, whoever does not receive the kingdom of God like a child will not enter it at all.

God is birthing His Kingdom, but only those who receive it with the innocence, acceptance, and lack of judgment of a child can enter. Praying in the Spirit births a childlike heart.

Why do we always have to try to figure out and make sense of everything God is doing? Rather than rely upon our intellect, we should search the Scriptures to discover if a thing is true. God hides what He is doing for true seekers to find. Some say, "You must be careful thinking the Holy Spirit will speak to you about supernatural things; it can be deceptive." However, it is only deceptive if we try to figure God out with our carnal understanding. When we walk in close relationship with the Holy Spirit, He will keep us from error.

The Genesis of Carnal Understanding

The eyes of mankind's carnal understanding were opened when Adam and Eve listened to the wrong voice and bit into the wrong fruit. Instead of seeking God's voice, they chose to believe the voice of reasoning, the voice of the enemy. Previously, they had seen things as God saw them and used spiritual discernment. In John 9:39, Jesus said:

> For judgment I came into this world, so that those who do not see may see, and that those who see may become blind.

God wants us to see once again with our spiritual eyes and discernment, and to become blind to our carnal vision and comprehension.

Paul contrasted the spiritual mind with the carnal mind in his writing to the Corinthian church:

> Now we have received, not the spirit of the world, but the Spirit who is from God, so that we may know the things freely given to us by God, which things we also speak, not in words taught by human wisdom, but in those taught by the Spirit, combining spiritual thoughts with spiritual words (1 Corinthians 2:12–13).

There are many important truths in this portion of Scripture; however, I want to focus on its application concerning tongues.

When you pray in tongues, you are speaking mysteries of the Kingdom in a spiritual language.

Paul goes on to say that when we think with our spirit, drawing from the mysteries and revelations that come from our spirit, we are operating in the "mind of Christ." Our minds are no longer error centers but redeemed to think and comprehend

When you pray in tongues, you are speaking mysteries of the Kingdom in a spiritual language.

with the mind of Christ. Here is how Paul summed it up:

> Those who are spiritual can evaluate all things, but they themselves cannot be evaluated by others ... But we understand these things, for we have the mind of Christ (1 Corinthians 2:15–16 NLT).

By praying in tongues, you are better able to discern accurately the things that come to your attention, because the "mind of Christ" is greater than natural understanding. It draws from the Spirit and heavenly truth.

A "WORD" FOR YOU

> I prophesy that if you will begin praying in tongues regularly for extended periods, things will shift for you. There are future revivalists, world changers, and history makers reading this book right now who will be activated through praying in tongues. Seasons of praying in tongues are being released to you as you read these words.

All creation is groaning for the manifestation of the sons of God, who are led by the Spirit of God. Pray in tongues more and think less. We do not need more reasoning; we need God! We need God! We have the mind of Christ in our spirit; let us embrace it.

This is a new day! It is a breakthrough day for you, with new seasons, new releases, and new realms in which you can soar.

> *This is a new day! It is a breakthrough day for you, with new seasons, new releases, and new realms in which you can soar.*

Chapter 4

CAN *YOU* RECEIVE THE HOLY SPIRIT BAPTISM?

God wants everyone to speak in tongues; it is "normal" for born-again people! Paul said, "Now I wish that you all spoke in tongues" (1 Corinthians 14:5). Some people interpret this in a negative way, believing that Paul was just "wishing" everyone was *able* to speak in tongues when in reality they could not. However, Paul was actually expressing that everyone *can* speak in tongues and his wish was that they would all do so. His hope would have never found a place in Holy Scripture unless it was also a desire of God. This was later confirmed when Paul said that he spoke in tongues more than anyone in the Corinthian church (1 Corinthians 14:18). He wrote this because he desired for them to imitate him and learn from his example. Paul understood the value of this precious gift.

FAITH IS A MUST

My salvation experience was dramatic and powerful. I wept as I felt the presence of the Lord come into my life. I could sense my sins being removed and the infusion of new life. I cried all night long – it was a dramatic experience that forever changed my life. Some may have had a similar rebirth experience, but for others it may not have been so sensational. Yet the truth of regeneration is the same – it does not matter what you felt or did not feel. What makes the experience valid is your faith ... not your feelings.

When I received the baptism of the Holy Spirit with the evidence of speaking in tongues, I did not feel a thing! It was not dramatic like my salvation experience. I had read Dennis Bennett's book, *The Holy Spirit and You: A Study Guide to the Spirit-Filled Life*. (This is an excellent book on the person and gifts of the Holy Spirit.) At the end of the book was a little prayer to receive the Holy Spirit and be released into tongues. I prayed that prayer and I did not *feel* a thing – nothing at all ... no lightning bolts ... no goosebumps, nothing! I thought to myself, "Well, I read the book and did what it said to do and I did everything the Scriptures told me to do, so I guess I must have it."

The book told me to step out in faith and begin to speak in a new language as the Spirit of God inspired me, so I did. The word I spoke was somewhat strange and I thought, "I'm making this up; I know I am. I don't feel anything at all! My lips aren't swelling, my tongue isn't shaking, and my voice isn't quivering – nothing." I only had three little syllables: "en-ti-ki." I knew that I had to be making it up because it seemed strange, and yet somehow it also seemed normal.

Then I recalled a Scripture I read that morning in the book of Hebrews:

And without faith it is impossible to please Him, for he who comes to God must believe that He is and that He is a rewarder of those who seek Him (Hebrews 11:6).

I received the Baptism in the Spirit by faith and thought to myself, "Well, faith is what pleases

God, not my feelings. So, I'm doing this by faith. If He's pleased, that's all that matters." I continued repeating over and over the three syllables I had received as a prayer language. I repeated them everywhere I went, all the while never *feeling* a thing!

I talked to my pastor the next day and told him, "I received tongues!"

He said, "Oh, that's wonderful. Let me hear."

I thought with a sigh, "Well, here goes," and I said, my three syllables, "en-ti-ki."

He commented, "Oh, yeah, okay," but sounded doubtful. I did not allow his disbelief to ruin my walk of faith. I constantly fought the thought, "You're just making this up; it's baby talk. You're making a fool of yourself."

However, I knew I was chasing after God and continued repeating what I had received. I had read the Scripture that says if you are faithful with a little, God will give you much (Matthew 25:21-23). I knew I had to be faithful with my three syllables because I wanted more. I thought that maybe one day there would be an explosion of tongues in my spirit, and that is exactly what happened.

One day as I was driving my car, repeating my three syllables, saying them backward, forward, upside down and inside out; singing, talking, and even shouting them, a flood of utterance came forth with new words and syllables I had never heard before. Like a river released inside my spirit, water was now gushing forth. I had been faithful with little and God gave me abundance.

It might be only a drop at first or even a small trickle, but it can easily become a stream or a mighty, rushing river. Speaking of you, Jesus promised, "From his innermost being will flow rivers of living water" (John 7:38).

THE GIFT OF TONGUES IS RELEASED BY FAITH

No matter what you feel or do not feel, it is about faith, from beginning to end. You must believe you already have the Holy Spirit, the Giver of the gifts, living inside you, which means you have tongues already within, lying dormant. It is not an issue of whether you have it or not – you already have tongues, and it wants to come out!

> *The gift of tongues is released by faith ...*
> *so take a step of faith and let it*
> *come out of your spirit!*

Take a step of faith and let it come out of your spirit.

THE MIGHTY POWER OF ONE WORD

Some individuals initially receive only a word or a few syllables when they believe for the gift of tongues. However, do not become discouraged if you do not receive an entire language. A single word or a few sounds can be very powerful.

A few years ago when on a preaching tour in Europe, the moment I arrived in Amsterdam, I received a new word while praying in tongues. I had never spoken that word before nor had I heard it. I went throughout Europe saying that one word repeatedly. Every time I repeated it, I sensed an incredible power being released through me. I wondered what I was saying because God was touching people as I proclaimed that word.

When I came home from Europe, I was doing a prayer seminar when suddenly, in the middle of the teaching, I began declaring the one word I had received during the trip. A girl at the seminar told me she thought it was a Hebrew word.

I said, "Really, could you find out for me?"

She returned later to confirm that it is in fact a Hebrew word meaning "the God kind of life." I had proclaimed that word throughout Europe!

A month later, while doing a word study of the word "revival" for a conference, I discovered that the Hebrew word for revival was the same word I had pronounced over Europe. The full meaning was "the revival life of God!" God can release incredible power and blessings through one word.

One last thing about the significance of a single word: the angels who gather around the throne of the Lord utter only one word – *holy!* Obviously, that one word is enough to express who He is and forever will be.

Most often people discover that when they are faithful praying even with one word or a few syllables, increase comes over time. Never underestimate the day of small beginnings.

HIS WORDS ... YOUR VOICE

When God baptizes you in the Spirit, you are the one who speaks in tongues – not God! Some people have misunderstood and thought that when baptized in the Holy Spirit God takes control of their voice box and speaks through them. That has never happened and it never will! The fact is – the Holy Spirit gives you the language but *you* have to do the speaking. Although the Spirit is inspiring you with what to say, *you* make the utterance; *you* bring forth the sounds of the words by yourself.

In Acts, chapter 2, it says that when the Spirit came on the people in the Upper Room, *"they spoke with tongues."* THEY were the ones who spoke as the Spirit of God gave them the words. The Holy Ghost is not going to talk through your mouth. *You are God's mouthpiece.* I have watched people sit with their mouths wide open and their tongues hanging out waiting for God to speak through them in a tongue, but it does not work that way.

When I speak in the language of my understanding (which happens to be English), my brain tells my voice box and my mouth what to do to produce a word. However, when I speak in tongues, my mind is out of the loop and the inspiration for

> *People discover that when they are faithful praying even with one word or a few syllables, increase comes over time. Never underestimate the day of small beginnings.*

the words comes from the Holy Spirit. God promised through the psalmist, "Open your mouth wide and I will fill it" (Psalm 81:10).

Speaking in tongues is actually quite simple. All you have to do is begin to talk as you receive the inspiration: open your mouth, begin to speak by faith. Do not think or analyze, just do it.

OBSTACLES TO RECEIVING TONGUES

While teaching on this subject around the world, people have told me about their difficulties receiving this gift. If you have had a hard time receiving – you might think you will never get it, that it might not be for you, or feel that something is standing in your way – I want to explain a few

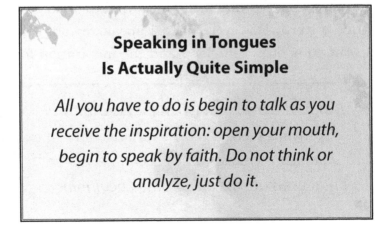

**Speaking in Tongues
Is Actually Quite Simple**

All you have to do is begin to talk as you receive the inspiration: open your mouth, begin to speak by faith. Do not think or analyze, just do it.

obstacles that have blocked some from getting their tongue.

First Major Obstacle – many people have received bad teaching about tongues. They have been told that tongues are not for today but ended with the apostles. This bad doctrine is due to a faulty interpretation of 1 Corinthians 13:10: *"But when the perfect comes, the partial* [referring to the gifts of the Spirit just outlined in the previous chapter] *will be done away."* They interpret the word "perfect" to mean when the Scriptures are completed; therefore, they reason, we do not need the supernatural today because we have the perfect Scriptures.

Actually, Paul was referring to the second coming of Christ and the new heavens and new earth when he used the word "perfect." We are still in the age of the Kingdom of God, the church age. Though the Scriptures are inerrant and needed for Kingdom living, they will never replace Jesus Christ. Only He is perfect and it is only when He returns to earth that the gifts of the Spirit will no longer be needed, because we will have Him! "For now we see in a mirror dimly, but then face to face" (1 Corinthians 13:12).

Cessationists believe that when the last apostle died, the gifts of the Spirit, including tongues, ceased to exist. That means that those with the gifts of the Spirit (which would have been most early believers) woke up the day after the last apostle died to find their gifts had been repossessed. That is obviously ridiculous. Tongues have not ceased, but much of the church has ceased believing in them!

Second Major Obstacle – the teaching that speaking in tongues is of the devil. Nobody wants to be partnered with the devil! This heresy is a logical outcome for those who believe the first obstacle that tongues have ceased. They conclude that if people are speaking in tongues today, it must be the devil's imitation. If either of these two doctrines is in the back of your mind, they will make you fear tongues. Faith is required to receive this gift and faith is not possible when fear is present.

Third Major Obstacle – the fear to speak something you do not understand. Some think, "What if I speak in tongues, and say something profane? What if I blaspheme God?"

Let me reassure you: that can never happen when you desire God's gifts. Would God give you something evil when you ask for His gifts? Certainly not, you can have absolute assurance that God can only give you that which is holy, pure, and lovely.

Some may fear getting a "counterfeit tongue" from the enemy. You might wonder if there is such a thing as a counterfeit tongue. The answer is yes, the devil counterfeits everything God does. He counterfeits prayer, worship, and everything else in the Kingdom of God. How do you receive a counterfeit tongue? You have to join the local witch coven or ask a demon for a tongue. You can never get a counterfeit tongue when your heart is right and you are seeking God for the "real thing." We have given our hearts to Him and been sanctified (set apart) for His glory and His purposes. We get the real thing when we ask Him for it! Our God is a good God and only gives good gifts to His children. He will never give you something evil when you ask for something good. This statement is true and bears repeating: *God is good and can only give good gifts!*

James said it like this:

Every good thing given and every perfect gift is from above, coming down from the Father of lights, with whom there is no variation or shifting shadow (James 1:17).

He was echoing what Jesus taught His disciples:

Now suppose one of you fathers is asked by his son for a fish; he will not give him a snake instead of a fish, will he? Or if he is asked for an egg, he will not give him a scorpion, will he? If you then, being evil, know how to give good gifts to your children, how much more will your heavenly Father give the Holy Spirit to those who ask Him? (Luke 11:11–13).

You may need to renounce the fears and hindrances that come from wrong theology and bad doctrine. Friends, each of you were created for a

Our God is a good God and only gives good gifts to His children.
He will never give you something evil when you ask for something good.

divine purpose and God is waiting to release His glory through you. You merely have to step out in faith to activate the gift of tongues that already resides within you. Do it today!

ABC's of the Holy Spirit Baptism

In the book, *The Holy Spirit and You: A Study Guide to the Spirit-Filled Life*, Dennis and Rita Bennett speak of the ABC's of receiving the baptism in the Spirit. Using their guide, you can be baptized in the Holy Spirit *right now*! Here are the ABC's of the baptism of the Spirit in their words:

A. **Ask** Jesus to baptize you in the Holy Spirit. The book of James says: "You have not, because you ask not" (James 4:2). God gave you a free will and will never take it away. He won't force His blessings upon you, as this is not the way of Love. You must ask.

B. **Believe** you receive the moment you ask. "Ask, and you *shall* receive that your joy may be full" (John 16:24). Faith is present-tense belief. "*Now faith is ...*" says the writer of Hebrews (Hebrews 11:1). Faith is also active and not passive, which means you must take the first step.

C. Confess with your lips. When you received Jesus as Savior, you believed in your heart and confessed Him with your lips. Now confess with your lips, but in a new language that the Lord is ready to give you. Open your mouth and show that you believe the Lord has baptized you in the Spirit by *beginning to speak*. Don't speak English or any other language you know, for God can't guide you to speak in tongues if you are speaking in a language known to you. You can't speak two languages at once! Trust God to give you the words, just as Peter trusted Jesus to let him walk on the water. Speaking in tongues is a childlike act of faith. It involves no ability, but rather the setting aside of ability. It is simply speaking, using your voice, but instead of saying what your mind wants to say, you trust the Holy Spirit to guide your voice directly to say what He wants you to say.[1]

TAKE THE LEAP OF FAITH

Why not take the plunge? Invite the Holy Spirit to fill you to overflowing, saturating you with His presence. Receive by faith the gift of tongues and then spend time every day praying in your new language – try praying in tongues for at least one hour every day. Then watch the supernatural begin to occur in your life. Your prayer life will become more vibrant, your witnessing more powerful, you will receive supernatural help in your workplace and every area of life, and you will gain a new boldness and confidence. You will have increased faith to perform miracles and healings as God leads you. Divine appointments will become more frequent as you witness a new measure of grace in your life.

The gift of tongues is truly a blessing from God. If you have already been released in your prayer language but you have put it on the shelf and not utilized this glorious grace, then now is the time to rise up and pray, pray, pray.

It is a new day for you. Enjoy the empowerment and accelerated faith and maturity this gift offers you. Cuma-shun-dai!

[1] Dennis & Rita Bennett, *The Holy Spirit and You: A Study Guide to the Spirit-Filled Life* (South Plainfield, NJ: Bridge Publishing Inc., 1971), pg. 69.

About Patricia King

Patricia King is a respected apostolic minister of the gospel and has been a pioneering voice in ministry, serving for over 30 years as a Christian minister in conference speaking, prophetic service, church leadership, and television and radio appearances. She is the founder of Patricia King Ministries, Women in Ministry Network and Patricia King Institute, the co-founder of XPmedia.com, and director of Women on the Frontlines. She has written many books, produced numerous CDs and DVDs, and hosts her TV program, *Patricia King – Everlasting Love TV*. She is also a successful business owner and an inventive entrepreneur. Patricia's reputation in the Christian community is world-renowned.

To Connect:

Patricia King website: PatriciaKing.com

Facebook: Facebook.com/PatriciaKingPage

Patricia King Institute: PatriciaKingInstitute.com

Women on the Frontlines and Women in Ministry Network: Woflglobal.com

Patricia King – Everlasting Love TV show and many other video teachings by Patricia: XPmedia.com

You've Been Given Ears That Hear!

Do you desire to hear what God is saying in this hour? Are you crying out for the Lord to speak to you about the deep mysteries of His Kingdom? Do you wonder what His plans are for your life? Then you need ears that hear!

In *Ears that Hear*, you will come to know that you, too, can hear God's voice. You will learn simple and practical ways to step into the prophetic and to begin listening to what the Lord is saying.

You've Been Given Eyes that See!

Do you desire to see into the unseen realm? Are you longing to gaze upon Jesus and His Kingdom? Then you need eyes that see!

Eyes that See will help you lay hold of the spiritual sight that you have been given in Christ. You will see in Scripture that the Lord has opened your eyes, and you will learn simple and practical ways to begin practicing seeing in the Spirit.

Available at PatriciaKing.com and Amazon.com

Decree a thing and it shall be established.
Job 22:28

The Word of God is powerful and it will profoundly influence your life. It does not return void, but accomplishes everything that it is sent to do. Patricia King wrote this book to help believers activate the power of the Word in key areas of their lives, including health, provision, love, glory, blessing, favor, victory, wisdom, family, business, spiritual strength and many others.

DEVELOP YOUR FIVE SPIRITUAL SENSES

Hear, see, taste, smell and touch the invisible world around you. We already know we have five five physical senses that are hearing, seeing, tasting, smelling and touching. But were you aware that we have five parallel senses in the Spirit? In this book, Patricia shares from her wealth of experience and revelation to help you understand your five spiritual senses and how to develop them. It is not just about knowledge, it is a doorway to encounter.

Additional copies of this book and other
book titles from Patricia King are available at:

Amazon.com
PatriciaKing.com

Bulk/wholesale prices for stores and ministries:

Please contact: resource@patriciaking.com

Patricia King Enterprises